PLAY & LEARN
WITH MAGNETS

Written by Gayle Bittinger
Illustrated by Gary Mohrmann

TOTLINE®
BOOKS

Warren Publishing House, Inc.
Everett, Washington

We wish to acknowledge the following teachers, parents, and child-care workers who contributed ideas to this book: Allyson Baernstein, Newark, DE; Betty Ruth Baker, Waco, TX; Janice Bodenstedt, Jackson, MI; Rosemary Giordano, Philadelphia, PA; Micky Goorman, Cincinnati, OH; Maureen Gutyan, Williams Lake, B.C.; Gemma Hall-Hart, Bellingham, WA; Margo Miller, Westerville, OH; Susan M. Paprocki, Northbrook, IL; Bev Qualheim, Marquette, MI; Betty Silkunas, Lansdale, PA; Diane Thom, Maple Valley, WA.

EDITORIAL STAFF:
    Editorial Manager: Kathleen Cubley
    Editors: Susan Hodges, Elizabeth McKinnon,
     Jean Warren
    Copy Editor: Miriam Bulmer
    Proofreader: Mae Rhodes
    Editorial Assistant: Erica West

DESIGN AND PRODUCTION STAFF:
    Art Manager: Jill Lustig
    Book Design/Layout: Lynne Faulk, Sarah Ness
    Cover Design: Brenda Mann Harrison, Mae Rhodes
    Cover Illustration: Kathy Kotomaimoce
    Production Manager: Jo Anna Brock

ISBN 0-911019-92-8

Library of Congress Catalog Number 93-61084
Printed in the United States of America
Published by: Warren Publishing House, Inc.
        P.O. Box 2250
        Everett, WA 98203

20 19 18 17 16 15 14 13 12 11 10 9 8 7 6 5 4 3 2

INTRODUCTION

Playing and learning go hand in hand with young children, and that's why your children will love doing the activities in this book, *Play & Learn With Magnets.*

Learn how to make magnetic teaching games, language props, art projects, and science props with the ideas provided in this book. Discover activities for encouraging the development of language and storytelling skills, learning about letters and numbers, and creating art with magnets. Find out how to use magnets to create all kinds of inexpensive multi-usable teaching aids that your children will love to play with while they learn.

Then explore the world of science and magnets with the science experiments in this book. Help your children discover the properties of magnets, how they attract and repel, and how to make their own. And while your children are playing and learning, use the music and movement suggestions to reinforce their experiences.

It's fun and easy to introduce your children to the world of magnets with the activities in *Play & Learn With Magnets.*

CONTENTS

Learning Games   *6*

Language   *22*

Art   *34*

Science   *42*

Music & Movement   *58*

Resources   *62*

LEARNING GAMES

Novelty Magnets

Collect a variety of novelty magnets such as the ones you can buy at kitchen and variety stores or the freebie ones with advertisements on them. Collect more than one of each kind of magnet, if possible. Set out the magnets. Let your children take turns arranging the magnets on a metal surface. Encourage them to sort the magnets by type, count out a particular number of magnets and put them on the metal surface, or find matching magnets.

Plastic-Lid Magnets

Save the lids of plastic gallon milk jugs. Use a permanent marker to draw alphabet letters, numbers, or simple shapes inside the lids. Attach small pieces of magnetic strip to the backs of the lids. Let your children arrange the magnets on a metal surface. Encourage them to find familiar letters, numbers, or shapes.

Earring Magnets

Start a collection of single earrings and earrings that you no longer wear. Use strong glue to attach a small magnet to the back of each earring (remove the posts from pierced earrings). Set out the Earring Magnets. Let your children sort the magnets on a metal surface by size or color. Have them select three or four magnets and arrange them on a metal surface in order of preference. If there are pairs of Earring Magnets, let the children find the pairs and place them side by side.

Button Magnets

Collect a variety of buttons. Attach a small magnet to the back of each one. Use the Button Magnets to create a pattern on a metal surface (red, green, red, green; large, large, small, small; etc.). Show the pattern to one of your children. Let that child sort through the remaining Button Magnets to find buttons to repeat the pattern below yours. Or let your children use the Button Magnets to create faces or other pictures on metal surfaces.

Color Shapes

Cut shapes (bears, stars, hearts, etc.) out of different colors of heavy paper. Attach pieces of magnetic strip to the backs of the shapes. Set out the magnet shapes. Ask your children to put just the red shapes, just the blue shapes, etc., on a metal surface. Or place different-colored shapes on a metal surface and ask the children to place matching colored shapes next to them.

Pan Shapes

Cut the following shapes out of heavy paper: squares, circles, rectangles, and donuts. Attach a small piece of magnetic strip to the back of each shape. Set out non-aluminum baking pans that are the same shapes: square, round, rectangular, and donut-shaped (an angel food cake pan or a tube pan). Pass out the magnets to your children. One at a time, have them name their shapes and place them on the matching pans.

Large and Small

Set out two stainless steel saucepans (one large and one small), large novelty magnets, and small novelty magnets. Let your children take turns sorting the magnets by size. Have them put the large magnets on the outside of the large saucepan and the small magnets on the outside of the small saucepan.

Inside and Outside

Give one of your children five or six different magnets and a non-aluminum baking pan. Give the child directions for placing the magnets on the pan such as these: "Put the square magnet on the outside. Put the pizza magnet on the inside."

Magnetic Puzzle

Cut a square out of heavy paper. Draw a simple picture on the square. Divide the square into four puzzle pieces by cutting it into four squares or four horizontal or vertical strips. Put a short length of magnetic strip on the back of each puzzle piece. Mix up the pieces and let your children take turns putting the puzzle together on a metal surface.

VARIATION: Make the puzzle out of magnetic canvas. (Magnetic canvas is available at some craft stores, or see Resources on page 62.)

Shape Puzzle

Select a non-aluminum pan (with an interesting shape, if possible). Cut a piece of heavy paper to fit inside the pan. Draw a simple picture on the paper and cut it into several puzzle pieces. Put a piece of magnetic strip on the back of each piece. Give one of your children the pan and the puzzle pieces. Let the child put the puzzle back together inside the pan.

VARIATION: Cut the shape out of magnetic canvas. (Magnetic canvas is available at some craft stores, or see Resources on page 62.)

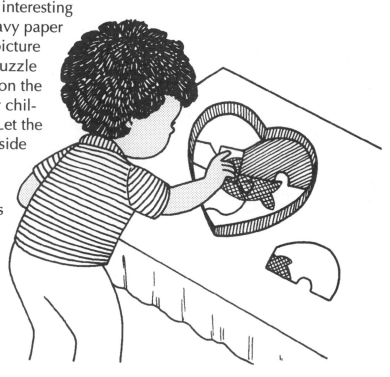

Magnet Picture

Collect several sizes and shapes of magnets. Arrange the magnets on an old non-aluminum baking sheet and trace around them with permanent markers. Remove the magnets. Use the permanent markers to draw a simple picture on the baking sheet that incorporates the tracings. Set out the baking sheet and the magnets. Let your children take turns matching the magnets to the appropriate tracings in the picture.

HINT: If desired, cover the surface of the baking sheet with plain-colored, self-stick paper before drawing on it.

Ladybug Spots

Cut five ladybug shapes out of red paper. Number the ladybugs from 1 to 5. Place the appropriate number of small round magnets on each ladybug and trace around them. Remove the magnets. Attach the shapes to a non-aluminum baking sheet with removable poster-mounting tape or double-sided masking tape. Set out the baking sheet and 15 round magnets. Let your children take turns putting the appropriate number of magnet "spots" on each ladybug.

Match-Up Game Board

Tape a column of clear plastic photo holders down each side of a large sheet of posterboard. Attach a brass paper fastener beside each photo holder on the left. Attach a small magnet beside each photo holder on the right. Tie pieces of yarn to the paper fasteners. Tie paper clips to the other ends of the yarn. Cut index cards to fit inside the photo holders. Draw pictures, shapes, etc., on one set of cards and insert them in the left-hand column. Make a matching set of cards and insert them in the right-hand column in a different order. To play the game, let your children match the cards by attaching the paper clips to the appropriate magnets on the right. Change the cards in the photo holders as desired to reinforce a variety of learning concepts.

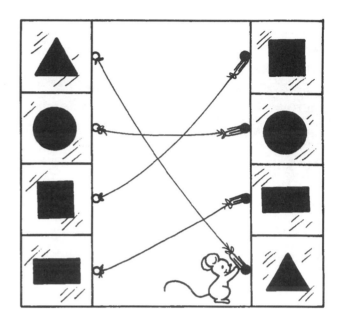

Coffee Can Game

Wash and dry a large coffee can and smooth out any rough edges. Cover the can with two or three colors of self-stick paper. Collect or make magnets in those colors. Place the magnets in the can. Let your children take turns removing a magnet and placing it on the matching colored section of the can.

Shape Wheel

Draw a circle on an old non-aluminum baking sheet using a permanent marker. Divide the circle into six sections. Draw a different shape in each section (a square, a triangle, a star, etc.). Then cut those same shapes out of paper. Cover the shapes with clear self-stick paper for durability and attach pieces of magnetic strip to the backs. Give your children the baking sheet and the magnets. Let them place the matching shapes in the appropriate sections.

VARIATION: Instead of matching shapes, match colors, letters, textures, numbers, etc.

HINT: If desired, cover the surface of the baking sheet with plain-colored, self-stick paper before drawing on it.

All Around the House

Use a permanent marker to divide an old non-aluminum baking sheet into four sections to make a simple floor plan. Label each section as a different room in a house such as a kitchen, a bedroom, a living room, and a bathroom. Cut out magazine pictures of objects you would find in each of the four rooms. Cover the pictures with clear self-stick paper for durability. Attach pieces of magnetic strip to the backs. Set out the baking sheet and the pictures. Have your children sort the pictures by placing them in the appropriate rooms.

HINT: If desired, cover the surface of the baking sheet with plain-colored, self-stick paper before drawing on it.

Matching Game

Select six pairs of stickers. Attach one sticker from each pair to a piece of heavy paper. Cut out the stickers and put a small piece of magnetic strip on the back of each one. Turn a 6-cup non-aluminum muffin tin upside down. Place the remaining stickers on the bottoms of the muffin tin cups. Set out the muffin tin and the sticker magnets. Let your children take turns placing the magnets on top of the matching stickers.

Tower Game

Cut a 1-inch, a 2-inch, a 3-inch, a 4-inch, and a 5-inch length of adhesive magnetic strip. Place the sticky sides of the magnetic strips on a piece of construction paper. Cut around the strips and place them on a non-aluminum baking sheet. Let your children arrange the strips to make a tower with the longest strip on the bottom and the shortest strip on the top. Or have your children arrange the strips with the left sides flush to make steps.

Fishing Game

Tie 3 feet of string to a paper towel tube, a wooden spoon, a ruler, or a plastic wand. Attach a magnet to the end of the string to make a fishing pole. Cut fish shapes out of construction paper, cover with clear self-stick paper for durability, and slip a paper clip over the top of each one. Place the fish shapes in a large box. Give one of your children the fishing pole. Let the child try to catch the fish by touching the magnet to the paper clips.

VARIATION: Cut various sizes of fish out of different colors of construction paper. Decorate the fish as desired. Ask your children to catch specific fish such as the big one, the red one, or the one with two dots on it.

Memo Holder Game

Purchase two magnetic memo holders (available at many kitchen, office supply, or variety stores) and a deck of ordinary playing cards. Attach one of the red cards to the front of one memo holder and one of the black cards to the front of the other memo holder. Put the memo holders on a metallic surface and place the rest of the playing cards nearby. Let your children take turns selecting cards and placing them in the memo holders with the matching colored cards.

VARIATION: Use the memo holder to sort plastic spoons and forks, index cards cut into shapes, or other small objects.

Magnetic Clip Game

Collect four magnetic clips (available at office supply stores). Select an activity, such as getting dressed, setting the table, or building a tower, and divide it into four steps. Draw each step on a separate index card. Put each card into one of the clips. Hang the clips on a metal surface in random order. Let your children rearrange the clips so that the illustrated steps are in the correct order.

Magnetic Board Game

Cover an old non-aluminum baking sheet with plain-colored, self-stick paper. Use permanent markers, stickers, or cut-out self-stick paper to create a game board as shown in the illustration. Set out three or four small magnets for game markers and one die. Select three or four children to play the game. Have each child choose one of the markers. Then let the children take turns rolling the die to see how many spaces they can move their markers on the game board. The child to reach the finish line first wins.

VARIATION: To make this a cooperative game, set a timer and have the children work together to get everyone's markers to the finish line before the timer goes off.

Crazy Cork Dancing

Make cork "dancers" by gluing plastic moving eyes and yarn hair on corks. Push a metal thumbtack into the bottom of each cork. Divide your children into pairs. Give each pair one of the cork dancers, a sturdy paper plate, and a strong magnet. Have one child in each pair hold the paper plate with the cork dancer on it, thumbtack end down. Have the other child in each pair hold the magnet under the plate so that it attracts the thumbtack. Have the children holding the magnets move them around so that the corks "dance." Then let the children trade places.

Magnetic Race Track

Find a large cardboard box and turn it upside down. Cut a *U* shape out of the bottom and sides of the box, as shown in the illustration. Cut 2-inch strips, slightly longer than the opening in the box, out of the cardboard. Securely attach the strips over the opening to make two tracks. Put a paper clip on one end of each track. Select two of your children to play the game. Give each child a magnet wand (or make your own by securing a magnet to the end of a ruler). Have the children hold their magnets under, but not touching, the tracks to move their paper clips. If desired, have them "race" their paper clips from one end of the tracks to the other.

Days-of-the-Week Magnet

Write the phrase "Today is" on a craft stick. On a small piece of heavy paper, write the days of the week in a column. Attach pieces of magnetic strip to the back of the craft stick and the heavy paper. Put the paper on a metal surface. Give one of your children the craft stick. Have the child place the stick in front of the correct day of the week.

Sunday
Monday
Tuesday
Wednesday
Thursday
Friday
Saturday

Number Game

Set out 20 craft sticks. Number 10 of them from 1 to 10 with numerals. Number the remaining 10 craft sticks with sets of dots from 1 to 10. Attach pieces of magnetic strip to the backs of the craft sticks. Place the sticks in random order on a metal surface. Let your children find the matching sticks and place them side by side.

Math Strips

Cut out a 16-by-16-inch piece of heavy cardboard. Collect 55 metal washers, all the same size. Cut a piece of magnetic strip long enough to hold one washer. Cut another piece to hold two washers. Repeat, cutting pieces to hold from three to ten washers. Attach the pieces of magnetic strip, in order of length, to the cardboard, with the bottoms of the pieces even across the bottom of the cardboard. Write the number of washers each strip will hold underneath it. Give your children the board and the washers. Let them put as many washers as possible on each magnetic strip. Then have them count the washers on each one.

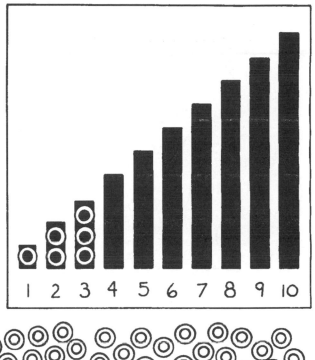

Magnet Math

Set out 10 to 12 different magnets and a non-aluminum baking sheet. Place two magnets on the sheet. Have your children count them. Then place three more magnets on it. Have your children count them, then the total number of magnets on the sheet. Take away one of the magnets and ask your children how many are now on the sheet. Repeat, letting your children add and remove magnets as desired.

Magnetic Numbers

Purchase plastic number magnets. Or, if desired, make your own by writing numerals on 2-inch squares of heavy paper. Attach a small piece of magnetic strip to the back of each square. Use the magnets in the activities on this and the following page.

Memory Game

Arrange two to four number magnets on a metal surface. Have one of your children look away while you remove one of the magnets. Sing the following song while the child guesses which number you removed.

Sung to: "Frere Jacques"

There is one, there is one
Number gone, number gone.
Can you tell me which one
Can you tell me which one
Is gone, is gone?

Gayle Bittinger

Number Matching

Set out several pairs of number magnets. Separate the pairs into two identical piles. Select one of the numbers from one of the piles and place it on a metal surface. Have one of your children look through the other pile to find the matching number and place it next to yours. Repeat with the remaining numbers.

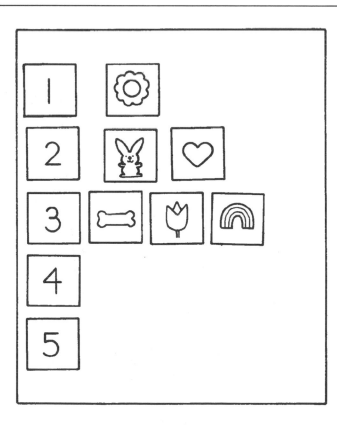

Number Fun

Collect 15 novelty magnets (or make your own by drawing simple pictures on 2-inch squares of heavy paper and attaching small pieces of magnetic strip to the backs). Select number magnets from 1 to 5 and arrange them in a column on a metal surface. Have your children place the corresponding amount of novelty magnets next to each number.

LANGUAGE

Magnetic Story

Collect a variety of magnets in novelty shapes such as foods, animals, miniature appliances, and people. Place the magnets in a bag. Set out the bag and a non-aluminum baking sheet. Have one of your children reach into the bag, pull out a magnet, and place it on the baking sheet. Then begin a story that incorporates the object represented by the magnet. Ask another child to select another magnet and continue the story until each child has had a turn or until all the magnets have been used.

Movable Story Characters

Let your children work together to tell stories with these Movable Story Characters.

Making the Characters—Cut pictures of people and animals out of magazines. (Cut the pictures so that the bottoms of the characters are flat.) Mount the pictures on heavy paper and cover them with clear self-stick paper for durability. Bend large paper clips into *L* shapes. Tape a paper clip to the bottom of each character so that it makes a stand. (See illustration.)

Using the Characters—Cut a hole in one side of a cardboard box and turn it upside down. Put one of the characters on top of the cardboard box. Hold a strong magnet and reach your hand through the opening in the box. Place the magnet under the paper clip on the character and move the magnet around. The character will move with the magnet. Show your children how to use the Movable Story Characters.

Paper-Doll Magnet Board

Purchase a set of paper dolls, or make your own. Cover the clothes for the dolls with clear self-stick paper for durability. Attach small pieces of magnetic strip to the backs of the clothes. (Some clothes may require two or three pieces.) Secure the dolls to a non-aluminum baking sheet with removable poster-mounting tape or double-sided masking tape. Set out the clothes and the baking sheet. Let your children take turns putting the clothes on and off the dolls. Encourage them to make the dolls talk to one another. Have them describe the clothing they are putting on the dolls.

Story Frames

Collect several inexpensive magnetic picture frames. (Available in several sizes at variety stores.) Cut out paper to fit inside the frames. Draw story characters on each piece of paper and put the papers in the frames. Place the frames on a metal surface. Let your children use the characters to tell stories. If desired, provide extra story characters so the children can replace them as their stories change.

VARIATION: Let your children draw their own characters on the precut papers.

Picture Magnets

Cut pictures of people, animals, and props out of magazines. Cover the pictures with clear self-stick paper for durability. Attach pieces of magnetic tape to the backs of the pictures. Let your children use the Picture Magnets to tell stories or with the activities on pages 26–28.

Greeting Card Magnets

Collect old greeting cards. Cut out the small animals, people, and objects pictured on the cards. If desired, glue the pictures to cardboard for durability before cutting them out. Attach pieces of magnetic strip to the backs of the pictures. Let your children use the Greeting Card Magnets to tell stories or with the activities on pages 26–28.

Photo Magnets

Set up a special area to take full-length photographs of your children. Have several hats, scarves, wigs, glasses, necklaces, and other props available. Let your children dress up in the props as desired. Take several photographs of each child. After the photos are developed, mount them on heavy paper and cover them with clear self-stick paper for durability. Attach pieces of magnetic strips to the backs of the photos. Let your children use the Photo Magnets to tell stories or with the activities on pages 26–28.

Story Magnets

Select one or two of your children's favorite stories such as "The Three Bears" and "Little Red Riding Hood." Cut the shapes of the characters and the important props out of cardboard, paper, plastic foam, or balsa wood scraps. Attach pieces of magnetic strip to the backs of the shapes. Let your children use the Story Magnets to retell their favorite stories or with the activities on pages 26–28.

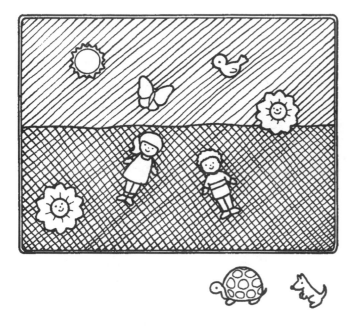

Scenery for Magnets

To make a land and sky scene, cover the bottom half of an old non-aluminum baking sheet with green self-stick paper. Cover the top half of the baking sheet with blue self-stick paper. Set out a variety of magnets (including the ones on pages 24–25) and the decorated baking sheet. Let your children arrange the magnets on the baking sheet to tell stories.

Magnetic Puppets

Collect several metal spatulas and story-character magnets (the ones described on pages 24–25 work well). Put one magnet on each spatula to make Magnetic Puppets. Make a puppet stage by turning a small table on its side or draping a blanket between two chairs. Let your children use the Magnetic Puppets and the puppet stage to tell familiar stories or to make up their own. Have more magnets available so the children can change the characters as desired.

Magnetic Stands

Collect a variety of sizes of metal bookends. Set out the bookends and story-character magnets (the ones described on pages 24–25 work well). Let your children place the desired characters on the bookends. Then have them move the bookends around as they tell a story with the characters.

Magnetic Flannelboard

Cut 18-by-24-inch pieces out of lightweight metal screen, flannel, and cardboard. Place the screen between the flannel and the cardboard. Use strong tape to secure the edges. This Magnetic Flannelboard can be used with magnets (the ones described on pages 24–25 work well), felt characters, or any combination of the two. Let your children place the characters on the Magnetic Flannelboard to tell stories.

Story Tin

Place several small story-character magnets (the ones on pages 24–25 work well) in a metal tin. Give the tin to one of your children. Let the child take the characters out of the tin and place them on the lid. Then encourage your child to make the characters talk to one another or tell a story with them.

Magnet Display Ideas

Magnets can be displayed and used on any metal surface. At home some ideas to try are the refrigerator, dishwasher, washing machine, dryer, microwave, or non-aluminum baking pans (baking sheets, muffin tins, pizza pans, etc.). At school you could try a metal file cabinet, a metal desk, a metal frame around a chalkboard, or metal doors. If desired, let your children help you find the metal surface for your next story or activity.

Eensy Weensy Spider

Find a large, round, black magnet. Cut eight short pieces out of black yarn. Glue the yarn pieces and two plastic moving eyes to the magnet to create a spider. Place the spider on a metal surface. Let your children take turns helping the spider act out the movements while you recite the nursery rhyme "The Eensy Weensy Spider."

Humpty Dumpty

Cut an egg shape out of heavy white paper. Cut the egg into three or four pieces. Attach a piece of magnetic strip to the back of each piece. Put the egg together on a metal surface. Recite the nursery rhyme "Humpty Dumpty" with your children. When he falls to the ground, have your children take the egg pieces off the metal surface. Let them try to put Humpty together again.

Magnetic Letters

Purchase plastic alphabet letter magnets in upper and lower cases. Or, if desired, make your own by writing letters on 2-inch squares of heavy paper. Attach a small piece of magnetic strip to the back of each square. Use the magnets in the activities on pages 30–33.

Alphabet Soup

Place six to eight letter magnets in a plastic bowl. (Use all upper-case, all lower-case, or a combination of both, depending on the skills of your children.) Set out the bowl and a stainless steel pan. Then let one of your children help you make "Alphabet Soup." Name one of the letters in the bowl, then have the child find that letter and stick it to the side of the pan. Continue until all the letters have been found.

Found a Letter

Place letter magnets in a box. Let one of your children pick out one of them. Have your child name the letter and put it on a metal surface while you sing the following song.

Sung to: "The Farmer in the Dell"

You found a *B* today,
You found a *B* today.
B, B, you found a *B,*
You found a *B* today.

Substitute the name of the letter that the child found for *B*.

Gayle Bittinger

Lining Up Letters

Set out pairs of letter magnets and two metal rulers. Arrange some letters on one of the rulers. Show the letters to one of your children. Have him or her find matching letters to place on the second ruler.

Letter Puzzle

Find an old, non-aluminum baking sheet. Use a permanent, wide-tipped marker to write upper- or lower-case letters the size of your letter magnets on the baking sheet. Set out the baking sheet and the letter magnets. Let your children take turns placing the letter magnets over the matching written letters on the baking sheet.

HINT: If desired, cover the surface of the baking sheet with plain-colored, self-stick paper before writing on it.

Matching Game

Collect a 6-cup non-aluminum muffin tin and three pairs of upper- and lower-case letter magnets. Turn the muffin tin upside down. Place the upper-case letters on the top row of muffin cups. Let one of your children place matching lower-case letters on the cups below the upper-case letters. Repeat with other letters.

Special Letter Game

Give each of your children a metal spatula and an alphabet magnet. Let the children put their magnets on their spatulas. Have your children tell you the names of the letters. Then sing one verse of the song below for each child, substituting the name of the child and his or her letter for those in the song.

Sung to: "If You're Happy and You Know It"

Katie's got a special letter, letter *C*,
Katie's got a special letter, letter *C*.
When you've got a special letter,
Things really can't get better.
Katie's got a special letter, letter *C*.

Rosemary Giordano

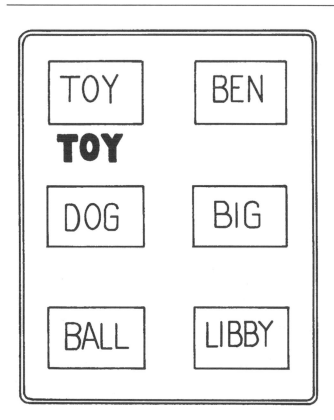

Word Fun

Write simple words on small index cards. Attach pieces of magnetic strip to the backs of the cards. Put the cards on a metal surface. Let your children name the letters that are in the words and place the matching letter magnets below them. Be sure to include the names of the children as well.

ART

Magnetic Painting

Drop small amounts of two colors of paint inside a large plastic box. Put a small magnet in the paint. Give one of your children another strong magnet. Hold the box carefully while the child moves the strong magnet underneath the box to make the small magnet move and spread the paint around. When the child is finished, press a piece of paper on top of the paint to make a print. Wash the box clean and repeat for each child.

Magnetic Picture

Draw a simple picture of a face on the inside bottom of a shallow box. Place some iron filings in the box. (Iron filings are available at some hardware stores, or see Resources on page 62.) Give the box to one of your children. Show the child how to move a magnet underneath the box to move the filings around. Then have the child use the magnet to arrange the filings on the picture to create hair, a beard, eyebrows, etc. Just shake the box to start over for the next child.

HINT: To keep the filings from spilling, cut a thin sheet of clear plastic (such as the plastic from a sheet protector or report cover) to fit over the top of the box and securely tape or glue it in place.

VARIATION: Instead of a face, draw simple scenes such as a forest, a beach, or the sky.

Magnetic Mosaic

Cut a variety of geometric shapes (circles, squares, triangles, etc.) out of colorful pieces of posterboard. Cut magnetic strip into small squares and attach one to the back of each shape. Set out the shapes. Let your children arrange the shapes on a metal surface to create designs.

VARIATION: Use ready-made plastic shapes, or cut shapes out of magnetic canvas of various colors. (Magnetic canvas is available at some craft stores, or see Resources on page 62.)

Magnetic Picture Frames

Cut sheets of magnetic canvas into fourths. (Magnetic canvas is available at some craft stores, or see Resources on page 62.) Cut a square out of the center of each fourth to create a picture frame. Give each of your children one of the frames. Have your children put on smocks. Then let them decorate their frames with colored glue, permanent markers, or puffy fabric paint. (Be sure to watch your children carefully as they use these products because they will stain.) Allow the frames to dry. Let your children hang up their decorated frames on metal surfaces. If possible, place a photo of each child in his or her picture frame.

Magnetic Necklaces

Collect the lids from frozen-juice-concentrate cans. To make each necklace, punch two holes in the top of one of the lids. Thread a length of yarn through the holes in the lid and tie the ends of the yarn together. Give each of your children a necklace. Set out a variety of small novelty magnets. Let your children arrange the magnets on the lids of their necklaces to make fancy pendants.

VARIATION: Make a Magnetic Belt instead. Punch four holes in each juice can lid, two at the top and two at the bottom. String the lids together to make a belt. Put a very strong magnet at one end of the belt for a fastener. Let your children take turns wearing the belt and decorating it with novelty magnets.

Magnetic Sculpture

Place a large, strong magnet on a table. Set out a container with small metal nuts, washers, paper clips, and other similar objects. Let your children take turns arranging the metal objects on top of the magnet to create a sculpture. Ask each child to describe his or her sculpture to you as it is built.

Clown Fun

Cut a circle out of construction paper. Attach the circle to a non-aluminum baking sheet with removable poster tape or double-sided masking tape. Cut clown hat, eye, nose, mouth, ear, and bowtie shapes out of construction paper. Cover the shapes with clear self-stick paper for durability and attach small pieces of magnetic strip to the backs. Set out the baking sheet and the shapes. Let your children take turns creating clown faces on the circle on the baking sheet.

VARIATION: Instead of a clown, attach a Christmas-tree shape to the baking sheet and cut ornament shapes out of construction paper. Or cut out the shapes of a basket and Easter eggs or a turkey and feathers.

Magnetic Devices

Collect a variety of magnetic drawing devices such as Magna-Doodle and Etch-A-Sketch (available at school supply and toy stores). Set them out. Let your children take turns using them to create pictures.

EXTENSION: Photograph your children's magnetic creations. Display the photos. Or put the photos in a book and let your children look through it to find their own artwork.

Gingerbread-Kid Magnets

Combine a 1-pound box of baking soda with 1 cup cornstarch in a saucepan. Gradually add 1¼ cups water and stir until smooth. Cook over medium heat, stirring constantly, until the mixture is thick and doughlike. Knead the clay on a tabletop and then flatten it. Use a gingerbread-kid cookie cutter to cut shapes out of the clay. Allow the clay to dry overnight. Give one of the gingerbread-kid shapes to each of your children. Let the children paint their shapes brown, then decorate them with glitter and sequins. Spray the shapes with clear varnish in an area away from the children. Allow the shapes to dry, then use strong glue to attach two small magnets to the back of each one. Let your children hang their magnets on metal surfaces.

Bagel-Face Magnets

Spray mini-bagels with clear varnish in an area away from your children. Allow the bagels to dry. Set out the bagels, plastic moving eyes, ribbon bows in various colors, and glue. Let each of your children select one of the bagels, two eyes, and one bow. Help your children glue the eyes on the top halves of their bagels. Then show your children how to put a bow on top of a bagel for a hair bow or on the bottom of the bagel for a bowtie. Let the children glue their bows wherever they wish. If desired, let them glue more than one bow on their bagels. Attach a magnet to the back of each bagel. Let your children place their Bagel-Face Magnets on metal surfaces around the room.

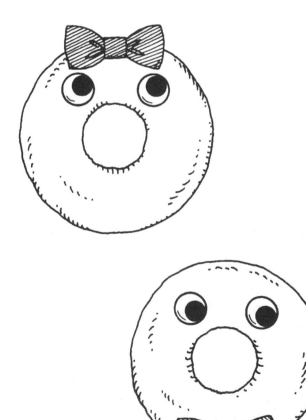

Harvest Magnets

Attach a piece of magnetic strip to the back of each of several small plastic lids (such as the ones from plastic gallon milk jugs). Give each of your children one of these bottle lids. Set out bowls of dried beans, dried peas, and popcorn kernels. Let your children glue an assortment of beans, peas, and kernels in their bottle lids.

Magnetic Display Clothespins

Give each of your children a spring-type clothespin. Let them paint their clothespins as desired. Allow the paint to dry. Using a permanent marker, write each child's name on one side of his or her clothespin. On the other side, attach a small, strong magnet. Let your children place their clothespins on metal surfaces. Show them how to display artwork and other papers from their clothespins.

Glitzy Pasta Magnets

Give each of your children a lid from a frozen-juice-concentrate can. Let the children glue assorted shapes of uncooked pasta on top of their lids. Encourage them to glue the pasta pieces as close together as possible. Spray the pasta-covered lids with silver spray paint in an area away from the children. Allow the paint to dry. Then attach strong magnets to the backs of the lids. Let the children hang up their Glitzy Pasta Magnets on metal surfaces around the room.

A Garden of Children

Collect a photograph of each of your children. Cut each photograph so it will fit inside a small plastic lid (such as one from a plastic gallon milk jug). Cut flower shapes out of construction paper. Give each child his or her photo, a plastic lid, and one flower shape. Have the children glue their pictures inside of the lids. Then let them decorate their flower shapes as desired with crayons or felt-tip markers. Then help the children glue their photo lids in the centers of their flowers. Attach a magnet to the back of each flower. Cut out construction-paper stem shapes and attach magnets to the backs of them. Let your children arrange the flower and stem shapes on a large metal surface to create a Garden of Children.

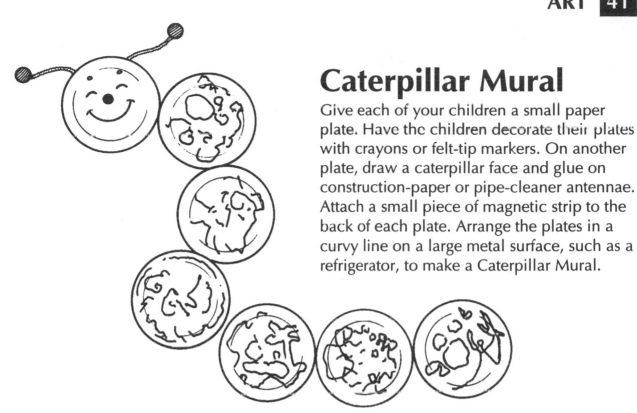

Caterpillar Mural

Give each of your children a small paper plate. Have the children decorate their plates with crayons or felt-tip markers. On another plate, draw a caterpillar face and glue on construction-paper or pipe-cleaner antennae. Attach a small piece of magnetic strip to the back of each plate. Arrange the plates in a curvy line on a large metal surface, such as a refrigerator, to make a Caterpillar Mural.

Dinosaur Mural

Cut the body shape of a stegosaurus out of construction paper and place it on a large metal surface. Cut small triangles out of paper and give one to each of your children. Let your children decorate the triangles as desired. Then attach a piece of magnetic strip to the back of each triangle. Let your children arrange their triangles across the top of the stegosaurus to complete it.

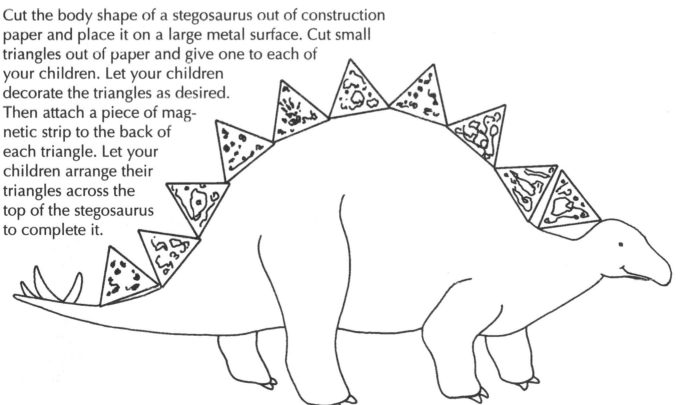

SCIENCE

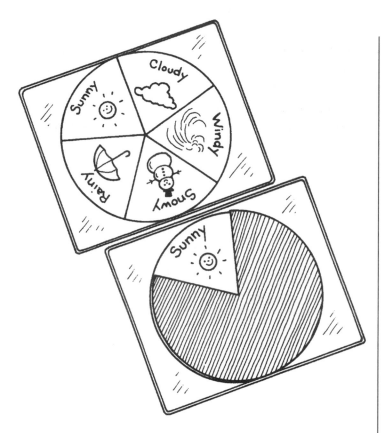

Weather Wheel

Use a permanent marker to draw a large circle on an old non-aluminum baking sheet. Divide the circle into five sections. Label the sections "Sunny," "Cloudy," "Windy," "Snowy," and "Rainy." Draw appropriate pictures in each section. Cut a large circle out of construction paper, the same size as the circle on the baking sheet. Cut one section out of it (so it looks like a pie with a piece missing). Attach pieces of magnetic strip to the back of the circle. To use the weather wheel, have your children tell you what the weather is like. Then have one of them place the paper circle on the baking sheet so that the section with the day's weather is the only one showing.

HINT: If desired, cover the surface of the baking sheet with plain-colored self-stick paper before drawing on it.

Four Seasons Tree

Use a brown permanent marker to draw a bare tree shape on an old non-aluminum baking sheet. Cut the following shapes out of construction paper: pink flower buds for spring; green leaves for summer; red, orange, and yellow leaves for autumn; and clumps of white snow for winter. Cover the shapes with clear self-stick paper for durability. Attach pieces of magnetic strip to the backs of the shapes. Give your children the baking sheet and the shapes. Ask them to decorate the tree in its "summer clothes," its "winter clothes," and so on.

VARIATION: Instead of cutting shapes out of paper, cut them out of magnetic canvas and decorate them as desired with permanent markers. (Magnetic canvas is available at some craft stores, or see Resources on page 62).

HINT: If desired, cover the surface of the baking sheet with plain-colored self-stick paper before drawing on it.

Plant a Garden

Cut pictures of vegetables and flowers out of seed catalogs. Mount the pictures on heavy paper and cover them with clear self-stick paper for durability. Attach pieces of magnetic strip to the backs of the pictures. Let your children take turns "planting" a garden by arranging the pictures on a metal surface. Help them name the different vegetables and flowers.

Bugs on Parade

Cut pictures of bugs (ladybugs, spiders, ants, caterpillars, butterflies, etc.) out of a science or nature magazine. Glue the pictures to heavy paper and attach pieces of magnetic strip to the backs of them. Draw an outdoor scene with grass and sky on a large piece of cardboard. Put a bug magnet on the front and a strong magnet on the back. Use the strong magnet to make the bug fly, crawl, creep, or dance across the cardboard while you recite the rhyme below, substituting the name and movement of your bug for the one in the poem.

Butterfly, butterfly, flying around,
Sometimes you're up, sometimes you're down.
Butterfly, butterfly, I hope you stay
So I can watch you every day.

Jean Warren

Rainbow Game

Cut a large half-circle out of heavy paper. Divide the half-circle into six sections as shown. Color the sections in this order from top to bottom: red, orange, yellow, green, blue, and violet. Cut the sections apart. Attach pieces of magnetic strip to the backs of the sections. Let your children take turns arranging the pieces on a metal surface to make a rainbow.

Ursa Major

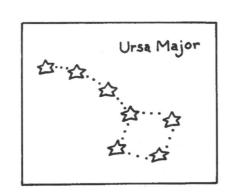

Constellations

Mount aluminum foil onto heavy paper. Cut small star shapes out of the foil-covered paper. Attach pieces of magnetic strip to the backs of the shapes. Cover an old non-aluminum baking sheet with black or dark blue self-stick paper. Set out the baking sheet and the stars. Tell your children that a constellation is a group of stars that has a certain shape and name. The Big Dipper (Ursa Major) is a constellation that looks like a ladle. Other constellations look like a swan, a bear, a fish, etc. If possible, show your children some pictures of constellations. Then let your children take turns using the stars and baking sheet to create their own constellations. Encourage them to name their constellations as well.

Body Puzzle

Cut the shapes of simple body parts out of paper (head, torso, arms, hands, legs, feet). Cover the shapes with clear self-stick paper for durability. Attach pieces of magnetic strip to the backs of the shapes. Place the shapes, all mixed up, on a metal surface. Let one of your children arrange the shapes to make a body. Encourage the child to name the body parts as he or she works.

Magnetic Graph

Find a large, old, non-aluminum baking sheet. Use a permanent marker to draw a grid on the baking sheet as shown in the illustration. Cut pieces of paper that will fit inside the boxes of the grid. Write your children's names on the papers, cover them with clear self-stick paper, and attach pieces of magnetic strip to the backs. Label the graph "Favorite Things." Cut out three paper squares that will fit at the bottom of the graph, and put pieces of magnetic strip on the backs. Select a topic for your graph, such as favorite apples, pizza toppings, games, or places to visit. If you are doing favorite apples, label each square with a different name and picture of an apple. Place the squares on the graph. Show your children the graph. Give each child his or her name magnet. Let the children place their name magnets in the boxes above the apples that they like best.

Favorite Things		
10		
9		
8		
7		
6 Alex		
5 Ryan		Shelley
4 Katie		Vanessa
3 Meghan		Alicia
2 Andrew	Jamie	Robert
1 Kailey	Rebeccah	Tom
red	green	yellow

Exploring Magnets

Collect a variety of magnets such as bar and horseshoe magnets, round and donut-shaped magnets, wand magnets, magnets in novelty shapes, magnetic marbles, and magnetic clips. (Many kinds of magnets are available at variety, office supply, kitchen, hardware, and electronics stores, or see Resources on page 62.) Also show your children a cabinet or box with a magnetic catch. Let your children explore and experiment with the magnets.

Exploration Jar

Put a handful of metal tacks in a plastic jar and screw the lid on tightly. Set out the jar and a strong magnet. While your children watch, hold the magnet to the side of the jar. What happens to the tacks? Remove the magnet. Now what happens? Let them take turns moving the magnet on and off the jar to make the tacks move.

Magnetic Strength

Collect a variety of sizes and strengths of magnets, including a large magnet that is not very strong and a small magnet that is. Set out the magnets along with metallic objects of varying weights. Let your children use the magnets to pick up the objects. Can all of the magnets pick up all of the objects? Which magnet can pick up the heaviest object? Can the biggest magnet pick up the biggest object? Lead the children to understand that magnets come in different strengths and that the size of the magnet does not necessarily reflect its strength.

Where Do Magnets Stick?

Explain to your children that magnets stick to things that are made of iron or steel. Show them two or three examples of iron or steel objects. Then give each child a magnet. Have your children walk around the room to discover places where their magnets will stick. Encourage them to test various surfaces. Will a magnet stick to a wooden shelf? To a tile floor? To a metal chair leg? When all the children have found places for their magnets, let them tell you where they put them.

Magnets in a Tin

Collect three kinds of small objects that can be picked up by a magnet (paper clips, screws, washers, etc.) and three kinds of objects that cannot (plastic buttons, small rocks, glass marbles, etc.). Set out a 6-cup aluminum muffin tin. Put one kind of object in each muffin-tin cup. Cut a thin sheet of clear plastic, such as the plastic from a sheet protector or report cover, to fit over the top of the muffin tin and securely tape or glue it in place. Set out the muffin tin and a magnet. Let your children take turns waving the magnet over the plastic to see what happens. Which items move when the magnet passes over them? Which items do not? Why?

Magnet Sort

Set out items that can be picked up by a magnet (paper clips, juice can lids, silverware, metal toys, etc.) and items that cannot (plastic balls, aluminum foil, paper, wood blocks, etc.). Mix up the items. Collect two boxes. Label one with a picture of a magnet and leave the other one blank. Have your children sort the items into the two boxes, putting the ones they think a magnet would pick up into the box with the magnet on it and the ones they think a magnet would not pick up into the other box. Then give them magnets to see if they sorted the items correctly.

Is It Magnetic?

Collect a variety of objects that can and cannot be picked up by a magnet. Make a data table as shown in the illustration. List the names of the objects you have collected in the first column. Show your children the data table. Read the name of the first object. Have your children predict if that item can be picked up by a magnet. If desired, ask them to tell you why they made that prediction. Write their prediction in the second column. Then hold a magnet to the item. Was their prediction correct? (Be sure to emphasize that learning from their predictions is more important than being "right.") Continue with the remaining objects. Encourage your children to discover the similarities between the objects that the magnet picked up and those it did not.

Is It Magnetic?

Item	Prediction	Actual
paper clip	yes	yes
aluminium foil	yes	no
spoon	no	yes
wooden block	no	no
cotton ball	no	no
metal washer	yes	yes

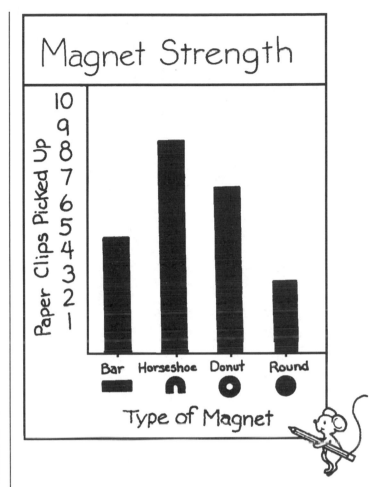

Magnet Strength

Paper Clips Picked Up

10 9 8 7 6 5 4 3 2 1

Bar Horseshoe Donut Round

Type of Magnet

Magnet-Strength Graph

Set out a variety of magnets and a box of paper clips. Make a graph as shown in the illustration. List the names of the magnets you have across the bottom of the graph. Let your children select one of the magnets and place it in the box of paper clips. Let your children count how many paper clips the magnet picked up. Find the name of that magnet on the graph and have your children watch as you make a bar up to the appropriate number on the left-hand side. Repeat with the remaining magnets. Have your children look at the graph after it is finished. Which magnet picked up the most paper clips? Which one picked up the fewest? Did any magnets pick up the same number?

Iron Filings Fun

Place small amounts of salt and iron filings in a flat, clear-plastic container. (Iron filings are available at some hardware stores, or see Resources on page 62.) Close the container securely. Give one of your children a strong magnet. Have the child hold the magnet over the container. What happens to the filings? To the salt? Let your children take turns using the magnet to separate the iron filings from the salt.

Magnet Search

Fill a large box or plastic bathtub for infants with sand. Hide a collection of objects in the sand such as a pencil, a small rock, a nut, a bolt, a washer, paper clips, coins, aluminum foil, keys, and a metal spoon. Let your children sweep through the sand with magnets to find the items that are attracted to it. Have them put those objects in a plastic bucket. Then let them take turns using a sieve to find the remaining objects and place them in a separate container. Encourage your children to describe the characteristics of the objects in each container.

Feel the Force

Set out a pair of strong magnets. Let your children take turns exploring the two magnets. Help them feel the magnetic force between the magnets by holding them close together. Ask them to discover how to hold the magnets to make them "jump" together. Then ask them to figure out a way to hold the magnets so they push away from each other. Explain that each magnet has a north and a south pole. When the north pole from one magnet and the south pole from another are close, they attract or jump toward each other. When two north poles or two south poles are close, they repel or push away from each other.

Magnetic Attraction

Collect donut-shaped magnets (available at many electronics stores). Make a stand for the magnets by inserting an unsharpened pencil into a large ball of playdough. Let your children discover how to put the magnets on the pencil so they are attracted to one another. Then let them put them on the pencil so that the magnets repel each other and appear to be suspended in air.

Magnet Swing

Bend a wire hanger so that the bottom becomes a point and you make a long, thin diamond shape. Then bend the hanger in half to make a stand. (See illustration.) Tape the bottom of the stand to a table. Tie one end of a piece of string through a donut-shaped magnet and the other end to the top of the hanger stand. (Bend the top part of the hanger if necessary to make the string stay in place.) Show the set-up to your children. Give one child a bar magnet. Let the child discover how to use the bar magnet to make the donut magnet swing back and forth without touching it. (Use the ends of the bar magnet to repel and attract the donut magnet.)

Magnetic Cars

Use masking tape to attach bar magnets to the fronts of small toy cars. Make sure that the magnets are attached so that some will repel and some will attract. Let your children play with the cars. Ask them to roll two cars toward each other. What happens? (Some of the cars are attracted to one another and some are not.) Can they figure out a way to push a car without touching it?

Magnetic Poles

Collect several square, flat, clear-plastic containers with lids, such as the kind you find at salad bars. Put a small amount of iron filings into each container and securely attach the lid. (Iron filings are available at some hardware stores, or see Resources on page 62.) Encourage your children to use bar magnets to explore the magnetic force of the magnets. Have them move the filings all around inside the containers. Then have them tape two bar magnets to a table end-to-end, with the like poles almost touching. Carefully put one of the containers on top of the magnets. Have the children observe the pattern that is made in the iron filings. Tape two more bar magnets to the table in the same fashion. Place another container over them. Is the pattern the same as the first? (It is.) Then tape two bar magnets to the table so that the opposite poles are touching. Place a container over them and let your children observe the pattern. Is it the same or different from the first two?

Tricky Paper Clip

Put a large glass filled with water on a low table. Have one of your children drop a paper clip into the glass. Ask your children to think of ways to get the paper clip out of the glass without putting anything in the water or dumping the water out. Then show them a strong magnet. Hold the magnet against the side of the glass until the paper clip attaches to it through the water and glass. Then slowly press the magnet up the side of the glass. The paper clip will come out of the water without the water being touched. Let your children take turns putting the paper clip in and getting it out.

Magnetic Trick

Preparing the Trick—Find a small box without a lid. Stand the box on its side. Attach a strong magnet to the top of the box. Use a pair of scissors to make a small hole in the bottom of the box, directly below the magnet. Tie a piece of string to a paper clip. Place the paper clip on the inside of the box so that it attaches to the magnet. Thread the string through the hole in the box.

Doing the Trick—Gently pull on the end of the string so that the paper clip pulls away from the magnet. The paper clip will appear to be suspended in air. It will not fall to the ground because the magnet is exerting magnetic force on it and pulling it back toward the magnet. The paper clip will fall only when it has been pulled beyond the force of the magnetic field. Put the paper clip back on the magnet and let your children take turns making the paper clip "float in air."

Stopping the Force

Collect five identical magnets. Set one magnet aside. Wrap each of the remaining magnets in a different material such as newspaper, fabric, plastic, or aluminum foil. Set out a container filled with paper clips. Touch the unwrapped magnet to the paper clips. Let your children help you count the number of paper clips it attracted. Then put the other magnets in the container to see how many paper clips each of them attracts. Have your children compare the numbers. Which magnet attracted the most paper clips? The fewest? Which material was best at stopping the magnetic force?

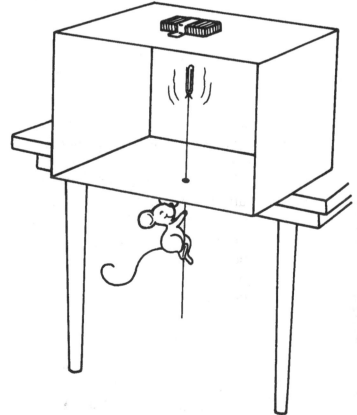

Lining Up the Atoms

Collect nine craft sticks. Use a blue felt-tip marker to color about an inch on one end of each craft stick. Show the sticks to your children, then drop the sticks on the floor. Explain to the children that objects that are not magnetic have *atoms* (tiny particles that make up the object) that look like the sticks, all mixed up. Then line up the sticks so that the colored ends are all pointing in the same direction. This is what the atoms in a magnet look like. They are all lined up. Let your children take turns dropping the sticks and lining them up.

EXTENSION: Explain to your children that when they rub a magnet in the same direction along a metal object, such as in the activity below, they are temporarily aligning some of the atoms in the paper clip to make it magnetic.

Making a Magnet

Set out a strong magnet and a box of paper clips. Tell your children that you can make a magnet out of a paper clip. Then straighten out one of the paper clips and rub it over the magnet in the same direction 25 times or more. Give the paper-clip magnet to one of your children and let him or her use it to pick up some of the regular paper clips. Then make a paper-clip magnet for each of your other children to experiment with. A paper-clip magnet is not as strong as a regular magnet, and its magnetic properties will eventually fade away.

Making an Electromagnet

Explain to your children that an electromagnet is a magnet that is made with electricity. An electrical wire is wrapped around a steel object, and when electricity flows through the wire, the steel becomes magnetized.

Collecting the Materials—To make an electromagnet, collect the following materials: a 6-volt lantern battery, 5 feet of electrical wire, a steel nail, two brass paper fasteners, a small piece of cardboard, tape, scissors or wire cutters, and a box of small paper clips or other steel objects.

Making the Magnet—Cut the wire into a 1-foot piece and a 4-foot piece. Remove 1 inch of the plastic insulation from each end of the wires. Push the brass paper fasteners into the piece of cardboard so they are about 1 inch apart. Put one of the paper clips around one of the fasteners. Attach one end of the 1-foot piece of wire to the other fastener. Attach the other end of the wire to one terminal on the battery. To the other terminal, attach one end of the long piece of wire. Leave about 1 foot of the wire free, then wrap it around the nail 25 to 30 times. Attach the other end of the wire to the paper fastener that does not have a wire. Tape the battery and the piece of cardboard to a table for security.

Using the Magnet—Move the paper clip so that it is touching both brass paper fasteners. This should complete the electrical circuit and magnetize the nail. (If it does not, check all of the wires to make sure they are securely attached.) Let one of your children put the nail in the box of paper clips. How many paper clips does it attract? Let your children take turns using the magnet to pick up other things. Make sure the paper-clip switch is turned off when the magnet is not used.

EXTENSION: The more times the wire is wrapped around the nail, the stronger the magnet is. Let your children experiment by wrapping the wire around the nail 20, 30, and 40 times, then testing to see how many more paper clips the magnet will pick up as the number of wraps increases.

Compass Fun

Explain to your children that a compass has a magnet in it to make it work. The north pole has a magnetic field, and the magnet in the compass is attracted to that field. So no matter where a compass is held, the needle in the compass will point to the north. Set out several compasses and let the children experiment with them. (Make sure the children hold the compasses somewhat apart or the magnetic fields will be disturbed.) Encourage them to make the needles move around. Then give them small magnets to hold next to the compasses. What happens to the needles? (The magnetic fields from the magnets are closer and stronger than the one from the north pole, so the needles on the compasses will point to the magnets instead of the pole.)

Making a Compass

Set out a straight pin, a strong magnet, a piece of cork, and a bowl of water. Magnetize the pin by rubbing it in the same direction across the magnet at least 25 times. Push the pin through the cork. Have your children watch as you place the cork in the bowl of water. The pin will point north. Let your children check this with a compass. Twist the bowl around; the pin will still point north.

North Pole

MUSIC & MOVEMENT

What Is a Magnet?

Sung to: "Yankee Doodle"

Do you know what a magnet is?
Go grab one off the shelf,
It's a stone or metal piece
That attracts things to itself!

Chorus:
Every magnet will attract
Iron, cobalt, nickel.
If you can remember this
You won't get in a pickle.

A magnet is a lot of fun,
'Cause things can stick right to it,
And you don't need tape or glue
Or sticky stuff to do it!
(Repeat Chorus)

When magnets pull, it's called attract,
Repel means push away,
And magnetism is the force
That makes it work that way!
(Repeat Chorus)

Margo Miller

Magnets Everywhere

Sung to: "Little White Duck"

There are magnets everywhere
Here and over there,
Magnets everywhere
Of this I am aware.
They stick to steel, oh, yes, it's true,
They're found in compasses and motors, too.
There are magnets everywhere
Here and over there,
Magnets everywhere.

Gayle Bittinger

I'm a Little Magnet

Sung to: "I'm a Little Teapot"

I'm a little magnet, watch me stick
To steel and iron, oh, so quick.
I'll stick right here, I will not budge,
Until you give me a little nudge.

Gayle Bittinger

Body Magnets

Have your children pretend that their fingers, elbows, knees, or toes have become magnets. Let them show you what would happen as they walk by a refrigerator or other object with a metal surface. Next have them show you what would happen as they walk by each other.

Pull and Push

Sung to: "Mary Had a Little Lamb"

Magnets like to pull and push,
Pull and push, pull and push.
Magnets like to pull and push,
Magnets are such fun.

Attract means pull, repel means push,
Repel means push, repel means push.
Attract means pull, repel means push,
Magnets are such fun.

Margo Miller

Attract and Repel Game

Explain to your children that they are going to pretend to be magnets. Use masking tape to make a "+" on the front of each child's shirt and a "-" on the back. Remind your children that a "+" and a "+" or a "-" and a "-" will repel (push away from) each other, and a "+" and a "-" will attract (pull toward) each other. Divide the children into pairs. Let the children in each pair discover ways to "repel" each other and ways to "attract" each other.

Looking for Magnets

Have your children leave the room. Hide a magnet for each child on metal surfaces around the room. Let your children come back into the room. While they are looking for magnets, sing the first verse of the song below. As each child finds a magnet, sing the second verse, substituting the name of the object on which the child found the magnet for *refrigerator*.

Sung to: "Clementine"

Look for magnets, look for magnets,
Look for magnets everywhere.
Up and down, all around,
Look for magnets everywhere.

Found a magnet, found a magnet,
Found a magnet over here.
Stuck right to the refrigerator,
Found a magnet over here.

Gayle Bittinger

Magnetic Exercise

On index cards, draw pictures of simple exercises, such as jumping jacks, hops, toe touches, and arm circles. Attach a small piece of magnetic strip to the back of each card. Set out the cards and a non-aluminum baking sheet. Let one of your children arrange the cards on the baking sheet. Then have all of your children do the exercises in that order. Repeat, each time letting a different child arrange the cards.

RESOURCES

Dowling Magnets
P.O. Box 1829
Sonoma, CA 95476
(800) MAGNET-1

Carries a large selection of magnets and accessories, including horseshoe magnets, magnetic strips, magnet wands, magnetic marbles, donut-shaped magnets, and iron filings. Call or write for the nearest outlet.

Magnetic Specialty, Inc.
707 Gilman St.
Marietta, OH 45750
(800) 848-6330

Specializes in flexible magnetic products, such as magnetic strip with and without adhesive, and magnetic canvas. Call for the dealer nearest you.

Crafter's Choice
11248 Playa Court
Culver City, CA 90230
(800) 421-6692

Carries strong magnets, and magnetic canvas in a variety of colors. Call or write for a catalog.

ChildWood
8873 Woodbank Drive N.E.
Bainbridge Island, WA 98110
(800) 362-9825

Specializes in magnetic wooden figures, magnet story boards, and curriculum for early childhood education. Figures come in sets such as community helpers, police/safety, family, farm, weather, dinosaurs, and several familiar stories. Call or write for a dealer near you.

Warren Publishing House, Inc.
P.O. Box 2250
Everett, WA 98203
(800) 334-4769

Publishes black-and-white and color pattern books for making magnetic characters easily and inexpensively. Available at school-supply or parent-teacher stores.

Totline®

Instant hands-on ideas for early childhood educators & parents!

This newsletter offers challenging and creative hands-on activities for ages 2 to 6. Each bimonthly issue includes • seasonal fun • learning games • open-ended art • music and movement • language activities • science fun • reproducible patterns and • reproducible parent-flyer pages. Every activity is designed to make maximum use of common, inexpensive materials.

Sample issue $2

Individual and Group Subscriptions Available

Super Snack News

Nutritious food, facts and fun!

This monthly newsletter features four pages of healthy recipes, nutrition tips, and related songs and activities for young children. Also provided are portion guidelines for the CACFP government program. Sharing *Super Snack News* is a wonderful way to help promote quality childcare. A Reproducible Subscription allows you the right to make up to 200 copies.

Sample issue $1

Individual and Reproducible Subscriptions Available

TWO GREAT NEWSLETTERS

from the publisher of Totline books. Perfect for parents and teachers of young children. Get FRESH IDEAS. Keep up with what's new. Keep up with what's appropriate. Help your children feel good about themselves and their ability to learn, using the hands-on approach to active learning found in these two newsletters.

Warren Publishing House, Inc.
P.O. Box 2250, Dept. Z
Everett, WA 98203

TOTLINE. BOOKS

Hands-on, creative teaching ideas for parents and teachers

Activity Books

BEAR HUGS. SERIES
Remembering the Rules
Staying in Line
Circle Time
Transition Times
Time Out
Saying Goodbye
Meals and Snacks
Nap Time
Cleanup

BUSY BEES SERIES
Busy Bees–Fall
Busy Bees–Winter
Busy Bees–Spring

PIGGYBACK. SONGS SERIES
Piggyback Songs
More Piggyback Songs
Piggyback Songs for
 Infants and Toddlers
Piggyback Songs in
 Praise of God
Piggyback Songs in
 Praise of Jesus
Holiday Piggyback Songs
Animal Piggyback Songs
Piggyback Songs
 for School
Piggyback Songs to Sign

1•2•3 SERIES
1•2•3 Art
1•2•3 Games
1•2•3 Colors
1•2•3 Puppets
1•2•3 Murals
1•2•3 Books
1•2•3 Reading & Writing
1•2•3 Rhymes, Stories
 & Songs
1•2•3 Math
1•2•3 Science
1•2•3 Shapes

MIX & MATCH PATTERNS
Animal Patterns
Everyday Patterns
Holiday Patterns
Nature Patterns

CUT & TELL SERIES
Scissor Stories for Fall
Scissor Stories for Winter
Scissor Stories for Spring

TEACHING TALE SERIES
Teeny-Tiny Folktales
Short-Short Stories
Mini-Mini Musicals

TAKE-HOME SERIES
Alphabet & Number
 Rhymes
Color, Shape & Season
 Rhymes
Object Rhymes
Animal Rhymes

THEME-A-SAURUS. SERIES
Theme-A-Saurus
Theme-A-Saurus II
Toddler Theme-A-Saurus
Alphabet Theme-A-Saurus
Nursery Rhyme
 Theme-A-Saurus
Storytime Theme-A-Saurus

EXPLORING SERIES
Exploring Sand
Exploring Water
Exploring Wood

CELEBRATION SERIES
Small World Celebrations
Special Day Celebrations
Yankee Doodle
 Birthday Celebrations
Great Big Holiday
 Celebrations

**LEARNING &
CARING ABOUT**
Our World
Our Selves
Our Town

1001 SERIES
1001 Teaching Props
1001 Teaching Tips
1001 Rhymes

ABC SERIES
ABC Space
ABC Farm
ABC Zoo
ABC Circus

PLAY & LEARN SERIES
Play & Learn
 with Magnets
Play & Learn with
 Rubber Stamps
Play & Learn with Photos

More books in this series!

SNACK SERIES
Super Snacks
Healthy Snacks
Teaching Snacks
Multicultural Snacks

OTHER
Celebrating Childhood
Home Activity Booklet
23 Hands-On Workshops
Cooperation Booklet

Cut & Tell Cutouts

NURSERY TALES
The Gingerbread Kid
Henny Penny
The Three Bears
The Three Billy
 Goats Gruff
Little Red Riding Hood
The Three Little Pigs
The Big, Big Carrot
The Country Mouse and
 the City Mouse
Elves and the Shoemaker
The Hare and the Tortoise
The Little Red Hen
Stone Soup

NUMBER RHYMES
Hickory, Dickory Dock
Humpty Dumpty
1, 2, Buckle My Shoe
Old Mother Hubbard
Rabbit, Rabbit,
 Carrot Eater
Twinkle, Twinkle
 Little Star

Story Books with Activities

HUFF AND PUFF. SERIES
Huff and Puff's
 April Showers
Huff and Puff Around
 the World
Huff and Puff Go to School
Huff and Puff
 on Halloween
Huff and Puff
 on Thanksgiving
Huff and Puff's
 Foggy Christmas
Huff and Puff's Hat Relay
Huff and Puff's
 Hawaiian Rainbow
Huff and Puff Go to Camp

NATURE SERIES
The Bear and
 the Mountain
Ellie the Evergreen
The Wishing Fish

**Warren Publishing
House, Inc.**